Fun with Subtraction

Katie Peters

Lerner Publications ◆ Minneapolis

Lerner Publications
An imprint of Lerner Publishing Group, Inc.
241 First Avenue North
Minneapolis, MN 55401 USA

For reading levels and more information, look up this title at www.lernerbooks.com.

Main body text set in Memphis Pro 24/39
Typeface provided by Linotype.

Photo Acknowledgments
The images in this book are used with the permission of: © Chan2545/Shutterstock Images, p. 3; © Image Source/iStockphoto, pp. 4–5; © Julie Vader/Shutterstock Images, pp. 6–7, 16 (left); © Wavebreakmedia/iStockphoto, pp. 8–9; © Ixepop/Shutterstock Images, pp. 10–11 © Sergio33/Shutterstock Images, pp. 12 (cookies), 16 (center, right); © Liudmyla Matviiets/ Shutterstock Images, p. 13 (numbers); © ediebloom/iStockphoto, pp. 14–15.

Front Cover: © Sergio33/Shutterstock Images

Library of Congress Cataloging-in-Publication Data

Names: Peters, Katie, author.
Title: Fun with subtraction / written by Katie Peters.
Description: Minneapolis : Lerner Publications, [2024] | Series: Math all around (pull ahead readers - nonfiction) | Includes index. | Audience: Ages 4–7 | Audience: Grades K–1 | Summary: "Young readers will love learning subtraction, especially when there are cookies involved. This nonfiction book boasts engaging, full color photographs and leveled text, perfect for emergent readers. Pairs with the fiction title Any Shelter Cats Left?"—Provided by publisher.
Identifiers: LCCN 2023002082 (print) | LCCN 2023002083 (ebook) | ISBN 9798765608708 (library binding) | ISBN 9798765616345 (epub)
Subjects: LCSH: Subtraction—Juvenile literature. | BISAC: JUVENILE NONFICTION / Readers / Beginner
Classification: LCC QA115 .P4684 2024 (print) | LCC QA115 (ebook) | DDC 513.2/12—dc23/ eng/20230519

LC record available at https://lccn.loc.gov/2023002082
LC ebook record available at https://lccn.loc.gov/2023002083

Manufactured in the United States of America
1 – CG – 12/15/23

Table of Contents

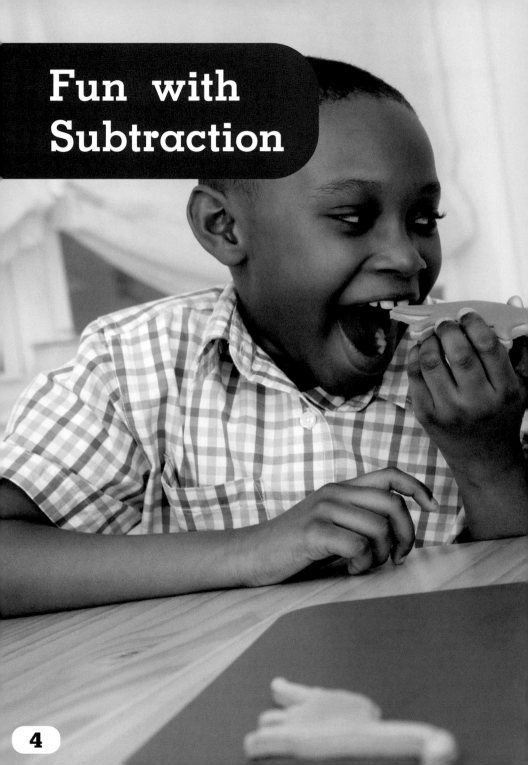

Fun with Subtraction

I can subtract. To subtract means to take away.

We have five cookies.

We eat two cookies.

Now we have three cookies.

$$5 - 2 = 3$$

Five minus two equals three.

Can you subtract?

Did You See It?

cookies

three

two

Index